"The privilege of a lifetime is to become who you truly are."

—Carl G. Jung

What Is The Intention Of This Journal?

This journal aims to understand and appreciate who you are using the personality type model. Intended to go deep to the core of your being and assess what makes you, you, how to accept and become the best version of yourself and reflect and jot down any plans, goals, or aspirations you may have.

Who Are The ENFJ's

ENFJ's use the cognitive functions:

Fe Extroverted feeling hero function

Ni Introverted intuition parent function

Se Extroverted sensing tertiary or child function

Ti Introverted thinking inferior function

What Does This All Mean?

Cognitive functions are mental processes.
Cognitive functions assist with:

- Attention
- Memory
- Language
- Perception
- Decision making
- Problem solving

According to Carl Jung, the mastermind of this framework, cognitive functions are:

"Particular mental processes or attitudes within a persons psyche that are present regardless of circumstances."

Carl Gustav Jung

How Does This Apply To Me?

Your Hero Function

Fe or extroverted feeling is your hero function for your personality type, meaning you have the most control of this function. It is something that comes so naturally to you. In most cases, it's your default, and you aren't even aware you are using it. Therefore, it is called the hero function as it leads the path for your whole psyche!

What Is Extroverted Feeling?

Extroverted feeling is an extroverted judging function. It is focused on group ethics and the collective feelings of others. This function strives for social harmony. High Fe users usually go out of their way to make others feel welcome and comfortable and are often the types that will break an awkward silence. However, high extroverted feeling types can sometimes neglect their own needs for the sake of others, making them very self-sacrificing.

Your Parent Function

Ni or introverted intuition is your parent function. This function is like the backbone of your personality. It keeps you upright and enables you to learn and make critical decisions. It's like the second brain for your hero function. Things often get filtered through the parent function in the decision-making process.

What Is Introverted Intuition?

Introverted intuition is an introverted perceiving function. Introverted intuition is internal pattern prediction. In other words, being aware of your own ideas and how they will influence your future. If healthy, this is a very entrepreneurial function. Introverted intuition develops many personal thought processes to dabble in and investigate in their own time. It enjoys gathering information and using it for its future. Many thought leaders are introverted intuition users for this reason. Introverted intuition is aware of sensory details because all introverted intuitive users use extroverted sensing. They use their extroverted sensing to understand current trends and happenings and later synthesize what they have collected to develop theories, trends, metaphors, and abstract interpretations of reality.

Your Child Function

Se or extroverted sensing is your child function, also known as the tertiary function. The Child Function is called the 'Child Function' for a reason. It has the innocent nature of a child. It often presents itself in an optimistic, larger-than-life kind of way. Another word often associated with the child function is the 'relief' function. You will tend to lean on this function when you feel most comfortable and relaxed. It's also an indication of how we like to be comforted. The downside to the child function is that it has a very temperamental nature. In other words, it's pretty easy to hurt someone's feelings if you say or do something to hurt the child function directly. Nevertheless, the child Function plays a vital role as it enables you to reconnect with your inner child and seek out the happiness you deserve.

What Is Extroverted Sensing?

Extroverted sensing is an extroverted perceiving function. This function does very well in situations where improvising for practical situations comes into play. Extroverted sensing prefers to live in the moment off of impulse instead of thinking about the future. Extroverted sensing is a very realistic cognitive function. People with extroverted sensing hero or parent functions are often great at bringing things back down to earth and showing things for what they truly are in the immediate moment.

Your Inferior Function

Ti or introverted thinking is your inferior function. Which is often suppressed in the ego. You will either try to hide it or run away with the responsibilities associated with it. As a result, many of your insecurities may be held in the inferior function. This function is hard to accept as we are fully aware of its downfalls, yet we feel we have little to no control over them. The key to success and self-integration is to master the inferior function. This can be achieved by volunteering to tackle tasks requiring a lot of its attention. Once you have a firm grasp on your inferior function, you can learn to handle its setbacks. Life then becomes more satisfying as you can become closer to harnessing your full power. Jung said that the inferior function was the entry to the unconscious or shadow self, the side of our personality that we hide from the external, and we may even be unaware of it.

What Is Introverted Thinking?

Introverted thinking is an introverted judging function. It is logical and conceptual. Ti likes to deduct logic and let the truth speak for itself. It relies on one's own analytical processes rather than statistics and external information. This makes Ti users very independent regarding their thoughts and opinions. I like to look at introverted thinking as a filter that eliminates false information until it can assess and break it down to its core meaning.

Journal Entry

Let's talk about your hero cognitive function of Fe or extroverted feeling.

The things associated with **Fe** have to do with:
- Creating and maintaining relationships with others
- Understanding and respecting the feelings of others
- Assuring everyone feels included and valued within the group
- Giving others opportunities to express themselves freely
- Taking the needs and wants of others into consideration and actively ensuring others needs are met

As an ENFJ, the above may seem like second nature to you. That's why we will use this space in the following pages to write out how you use extroverted feeling. Additionally, write how it impacts your life and whatever positives and negatives you have when dealing with the things associated with this function.

My Fe:

What are some goals or things you need or want to complete associated with Fe?

"You can be a good person with a kind heart and still say no."
—Anonymous.

Journal Entry

Let's talk about your parent cognitive function of Ni or introverted intuition.

The things associated with **Ni** have to do with:
- Personal ideas, visions, symbolism, and theories
- Insightful future ideas
- Understanding patterns and predicting trends
- Narrowing down to understand things to their core
- The unconscious

Ni or introverted intuition is your parent function. As stated before, it is like a filter for your hero function. We often assess how we feel about things using this function and depend on it to make decisions. Use the space in the following pages to write how you use introverted intuition. Additionally, note how it impacts your life and whatever positives and negatives you have when dealing with the things associated with this function.

My Ni:

What are some goals or things you need or want to complete associated with Ni?

"Intuition is the discriminate faculty that enables you to decide which of two lines of reasoning is right. Perfect intuition makes you master of all." —Paramahansa Yogananda

Journal Entry

Let's talk about your child function of Se or extroverted sensing.

The things associated with **Se** have to do with:
- Being present and living in the moment
- Living through the senses and experiencing life through them
- Being adaptable to your environment
- Being grounded and open-minded
- The freedom to experience life, taking bold risks, and thrill-seeking

Se or extroverted sensing is your child function. Look at it this way. The child function is not as well put together and mature as the other two functions. However, we tend to rely on this function when we are relaxed and like to engage in it while having fun. Use the space in the following pages to write how you use extroverted sensing. Additionally, note how it impacts your life and whatever positives and negatives you have when dealing with the things associated with this function.

My Se:

What are some goals or things you need or want to complete associated with Se?

"The purpose of life is to live it, to taste experience to the utmost, to reach out eagerly and without fear for newer and richer experience."
—Eleanor Roosevelt.

Journal Entry

Let's talk about your inferior function of Ti or introverted thinking.

The things associated with **Ti** have to do with:
- Classifying and labeling information
- Remaining detached and impartial when dealing with situations
- Problem-solving and coming up with new ways to make things work
- Using logic to deduct and critique information
- Listening to your internal thoughts and observations

Ti or introverted thinking is your inferior function. The things associated with the inferior function may seem the most foreign to you. However, once we learn to accept our inferior function, we can develop and learn from it. Use the space in the following pages to write how you use introverted thinking. Additionally, note how it impacts your life and whatever positives and negatives you have when dealing with the things associated with this function.

My Ti:

What are some goals or things you need or want to complete associated with Ti?

"No problem can withstand the assault of sustained thinking."
—Voltaire

The Importance Of Working on the Inferior Function

A lot of our insecurities are held in the inferior function. The inferior function is in the last position in our function stack. Therefore we have less conscious control over it, but we are fully aware of its downfalls.

Whatever your inferior function is, the things associated with it may be harder to grasp or unenjoyable/ stressful when doing something related to it.

The important thing about the inferior function is this function can be significantly developed and utilized for self-development! Tackling the more challenging, less comfortable things in your life is the key to success in any regard.

That is why the following journal entry will be focused on developing your inferior function.

Journal Entry

Working On The Inferior Function

Use the space in the following pages to write out ways you will be working to strengthen your inferior function.

Remember, the things associated with your inferior **Ti** are:

- Classifying and labeling information
- Remaining detached and impartial when dealing with situations
- Problem-solving and coming up with new ways to make things work
- Using logic to deduct and critique information
- Listening to your internal thoughts and observations

Ways I will strengthen my Ti:

How do you feel when you are confronted with things that have to do with Ti?

"What objectivity and the study of philosophy requires is not an 'open mind,' but an active mind - a mind able and eagerly willing to examine ideas, but to examine them critically."
—Ayn Rand

Journal Entry

Being an ENFJ comes with its unique benefits, and these are the things we have to be proud of when we look toward who we are. But, there is more to you than being just an ENFJ, of course!
Self-reflecting and noting down the things you appreciate and respect about yourself is essential in understanding and further strengthening who we are.

In the following pages, write out ten things you like about being an ENFJ.

10 things I like about being an ENFJ:

1.

2.

3.

4.

5.

6.

7.

8.

9.

10.

Why I am proud of myself:

"We accept the love we think we deserve."
—Stephen Chbosky

Journal Entry

The ENFJ benefits from writing out their goals. Therefore, it is good to write out all your goals on paper to become more tangible, making it more known that they are essential and are upon completion.

In the following pages in the designated spaces, write out your short-term goals, how you will achieve them and your long-term goals and how you will achieve them.

My short-term goals:

How I will achieve my short-term goals:

My long-term goals:

How I will achieve my long-term goals:

"A goal properly set is halfway reached." —Zig Ziglar

Journal Entry

Reach for the stars. There is no limit to the ability to live the life you dream of having.

The journal entry in the following pages is about having the free space to block out negative thinking and write out anything no matter how unattainable it sounds and enjoying the process of writing out your dreams. Once you flesh them out, you will find that anything is possible.

What would you do if you were granted unlimited money and resources right now? (Don't limit your thinking. This question is about limiting doubts and thinking as big as possible).

"The sky is not the limit, it's just the beginning." —Anonymous

Personality Type Log

Understanding the personality types of the people in your life is a great way to better understand them and how they work, leading to better communication and relationships with others.

In the space provided, use the following few pages to note down the personality types of the people you know.

Personality Types Of People I Know

Name   **Type**

_____   _____

_____   _____

_____   _____

_____   _____

_____   _____

_____   _____

_____   _____

_____   _____

_____   _____

_____   _____

_____   _____

_____   _____

_____   _____

_____   _____

_____   _____

_____   _____

_____   _____

_____   _____

_____   _____

_____   _____

Personality Types Of People I Know

Name   Type

_____   _____

_____   _____

_____   _____

_____   _____

_____   _____

_____   _____

_____   _____

_____   _____

_____   _____

_____   _____

_____   _____

_____   _____

_____   _____

_____   _____

_____   _____

_____   _____

_____   _____

_____   _____

_____   _____

Personality Types Of People I Know

Name

Type

_____   _____

_____   _____

_____   _____

_____   _____

_____   _____

_____   _____

_____   _____

_____   _____

_____   _____

_____   _____

_____   _____

_____   _____

_____   _____

_____   _____

_____   _____

_____   _____

_____   _____

_____   _____

_____   _____

_____   _____

Continue using this journal to note down additional personal goals, daily affirmations, events, or anything you like. If you have space in the above sections, feel free to elaborate or add more to your answers.

Happy Journaling

"We meet ourselves time and again
in a thousand disguises on the path
of life."

—Carl G. Jung

Printed in Great Britain
by Amazon